IT WILL STAND: STUDENT'S BOOK

In Home Bible Study for Teens

MARY LOVE EYSTER, WEETY VICKERY

WestBow
PRESS
A DIVISION OF THOMAS NELSON

All scripture taken from The Adventure Bible: A Study Bible for Kids. Copyright 1989 by The Zondervan Corporation.

The Holy Bible, New International Version Copyright 1973, 1978, 1984 by International Bible Society

WestBow Press books may be ordered through booksellers or by contacting:

WestBow Press
A Division of Thomas Nelson
1663 Liberty Drive
Bloomington, IN 47403
www.westbowpress.com
1-(866) 928-1240

ISBN: 978-1-4497-3192-2 (sc)

Library of Congress Control Number: 2011960686

Printed in the United States of America

WestBow Press rev. date:1/12/2012

Contents

With devotion always to our spiritual leader,

John C. Eyster Sr.

Preface

Dear girls,

We live in an ever-changing world! My mother and I began in-home Bible studies for all three of my daughters when each was in the fifth grade, and they continued through high school. That was twenty years ago. We still hear how much it meant to some of our girls. I now have been teaching groups for the past eight years on my own. Isn't it amazing that the same Scriptures that were given to our ancestors are still relevant for us today? The Ten Commandments that were written on the stones and given to the Israelites impart the same instruction for us in our day-to-day living. The Scriptures are just as alive and helpful as when they were first given. I have found God's Word is like opening a treasure chest; so many pearls of wisdom await us if we only take the time to read and learn! Take a trip with me now as we discover what the Bible is "all about" and how it applies to you as an individual.

—Weety Vickery

PART ONE

The Bible, What's It All About?

LESSON 1

A DIVERSE BOOK WITH A COMMON THREAD

The Bible is far and away the best-selling book of all time. It has been translated into more languages than any other book. It is the most influential book ever written.

1) Why study the Bible? II Timothy 3:16

2) Why study the Bible together? Matthew 18:20

3) What are the two divisions into which the Bible is divided? The _____ and the _____ Testaments.

4) How many books are found in the Bible? There are _____ total.

5) What is the span of time that separates the end of the Old Testament and the beginning of the New Testament? It is _____ years.

The Bible is unique in its continuity.

Josh McDowell says, "Biblical authors spoke on hundreds of controversial subjects with harmony and continuity from Genesis to Revelation. There is one unfolding story: God's redemption of man." Josh McDowell, *Evidence that Demands a Verdict* (San Bernardino, CA: Here's Life Publishers, Inc., 1972, 1979) p 16.

Look up the word "redemption" in the dictionary. Write the meaning.

6) The Bible has some _____ authors from many different walks of life.

7) The Bible was written over a time span of approximately _____.
It was written on three continents: Asia, Africa, and Europe.

8) The original Scriptures were written in three languages: _____, _____ and _____. Through the years, the Bible has been translated over and over again into many different languages and versions.

The Bible is unique in its circulation.

The Bible has been read by more people and published in more languages than any other book in history. No other book has known anything that approaches this constant circulation. It has been estimated that as of 2007, approximately 7.5 billion Bibles have been distributed throughout the world—not including digital versions. The complete Bible has been published in over 450 languages, the New Testament in nearly 1,400 languages. Fred R. Coulter, *The Holy Bible in Its Original Order* (Hollister, California: York Publishing Company, 2009) p 10.

According to the Gideons, Wycliffe International and the International Bible Societies it is estimated that 168,000 Bibles are bought or given out every day.

The average American household has approximately four Bibles.

9) Many kings, emperors, rulers, and princes throughout history have tried to ban, outlaw, and destroy the Bible. Yet today, it is *the* _____ book of all time.

10) Why do you think so many people through the years have tried to destroy or discredit the Bible?

The Bible is unique in its influence.

Historian Philip Schaff wrote, "This Jesus of Nazareth, without money and arms, conquered more millions than Alexander, Caesar, Mohammed, and Napoleon; without science and learning, He shed more light on things human and divine than all philosophers and scholars combined; without the eloquence of schools. He spoke such words of life as were never spoken before or since and produced effects which lie beyond the reach of orator or poet without writing a single line. He set more pens in motion, and furnished themes for more sermons, orations, discussions, learned volumes, works of art, and songs of praise than the whole army of great men of ancient and modern times." Philip Schaff, *The Person of Christ* (New York: American Tract Society, 1913) p 33.

11) What became of some of the early men who believed in the importance of translating the Scriptures into their native languages? Some examples of these men are William Tyndale, Martin Luther, Casiodoro de Reina, and Thomas Cranmer.

The Bible's influence on these men must have been profound. They believed God's message had to be shared at any cost.

12) What did Jesus say about his "words" in Mark 13:31?

Art Project

Song of the Week: "Ancient Words" by Michael W. Smith (can be found online)

LESSON 2

SYNOPSIS OF THE BIBLE, PART I
GENESIS THROUGH EXODUS

The next few lessons are a review of the *entire* Bible. You will see the common thread that is woven throughout these sixty-six books.

Genesis—the book of beginnings! We see the creation of the world and plant, animal, and human life. It is in this book that we see the origin of God's fellowship with man; the first sin; and the birth of God's chosen people, the Jews, as a nation. The primary figures of the Jewish race are Abraham, Isaac, Jacob, and Joseph.

Creation—nothing orderly comes from chaos.

1) The first man was named _____, and his wife was _____.

2) It took God _____ days to create the earth and on the _____ day, he rested.

God made a contract (Gen. 17:2-4) with Abram.

3) Why might we call Abraham "Father Abraham"? Genesis 17:5-6

4) Why was his son Isaac so special to him? Genesis 21

5) What did God ask Abraham to do with Isaac? Genesis 22 _____

Thankfully, God spared Isaac, and he later married and had a son, Jacob, and grandson, Joseph.

6) Joseph's brothers were jealous of him as a child because he was his father's favorite. Do you remember the story of the special gift his dad gave him, a coat of many colors? What did Joseph's brothers do to him? Genesis 37

Family favoritism is never a good thing. It can lead to jealousy, hurt feelings, and possibly worse. Do you ever feel like your parents love your brother or sister more than you? You might ask your parents if they ever felt that way when they were young and talk about the story of Joseph.

It happened then, just as it does many times even today, that what the brothers meant for evil, God used for good. Joseph ended up forgiving his brothers, saving his family from famine, and bringing the Israelites to Egypt to live.

God could not use Joseph further without him forgiving his brothers. Do you think you could forgive such a thing if it happened to you?

Through the years, the brothers and their families grew to be a huge nation of people, and the Egyptians decided to make them slaves. They even went so far as to kill the newborn baby boys to keep the population down.

Exodus *What word does this word sound like?*

7) One mother went to great measures to save her baby. She hid him in a basket and floated him in the river. Who is this famous baby? Exodus 2 _____

8) How did God place the baby Moses into Pharaoh's house to accomplish the work he later had for him? Exodus 2:1-10

9) God later spoke to Moses in the burning bush and instructed him to

(Exodus 3:6-10)_____.

In Exodus 3:11 Moses asked, "Who am I, that I should go to Pharaoh and bring the Israelites out of Egypt?" Don't you know he was terrified for his life and wondered how in the world the release of the Israelites could even come about? Have you ever felt that you had a task that was just too large for you to even think about tackling? God's reply in the next verse, Exodus 3:12, is one we should remember: "I will be with you."

Song of the week: "The Hope of a Broken World" by Selah

LESSON 3

SYNOPSIS OF THE BIBLE, PART II
LEVITICUS THROUGH KINGS

This week we are going to pick up the pace a little since we only got to the second book in the Bible last week! We take right back up with the Israelite nation. They have left a life of slavery in Egypt and are establishing their new life in a new land.

Leviticus: God sets up the laws, sacrificial system, priesthood, and special feasts that were to be celebrated during the year. Henrietta Mears said, "One of the most important questions in life is 'How may an unholy people approach a holy God?'" Henrietta Mears, *What the Bible is All About* (Venture, CA: Regal Books, 1983) p 52. At the very beginning of the book, we see God making provision for his people to approach him in worship. Sin is no small matter, and dealing with it is of great importance to God. Take time now to read Leviticus 1. *Warning, this can be gory!*

Numbers: This book is simple enough; the Israelites are numbered. They entered Egypt a family of seventy and exited 430 years later a nation of some six hundred thousand men twenty years old and older, plus women and children, an estimated total of some two to three million people. These people murmured and complained and rebelled against God and as a result failed to enter the promised land of Canaan at their first opportunity. They learned the hard lesson that punishment follows disobedience. It took them forty years to make an eleven-day journey.

Punishment followed disobedience. Is this still true today? Think of examples.

Moses was not without punishment himself. In Numbers 20, God instructed him to speak to a rock so that it would pour out water. Moses did not follow God's instructions. He struck the rock instead, and therefore he was not allowed to enter the Promised Land. Does this punishment seem a bit severe to you? Does it show us how serious God is about sin?

Deuteronomy: This word means "repetition of the law." At the end of their long journey, the Israelites were ready to enter Canaan, the land that God had promised to Abraham and his descendents. Moses was about to die, so he gave final instructions to the people he had guided for the forty years. He reminded them to obey God.

The next twelve books are history books, telling of the major events in the nation of Israel.

Joshua: This book tells how the Israelites entered the Promised Land and conquered it under the leadership of Joshua, Moses's successor. In Numbers 13 and 14, Moses sent spies into Canaan. Read Numbers 14:1-9 to see why Joshua was such a good choice as the Israelites' new leader. God had given them the land, but they had to possess their new possession. This is true in the spiritual realm as well. God has given us all great and wonderful promises, but we must claim them and live by them for them to become truly ours.

Treasure Chest Story

A man went to heaven and was shown a calendar of all the days of his life. On most of the days, there were unopened treasure chests. When the man asked what they were, God explained that they were treasures that were there for his taking. He just hadn't received them. How often are we so busy that we don't look for or receive the gifts (treasures) that God desires to freely give us?

Judges: The book of Judges tells how the Israelites would fall into disobedience and idolatry, and God would give them over to their enemies. Then the people would cry out to God, and God would send them a leader, called a judge, to rescue them. This cycle occurred seven times. The last verse in the book of Judges, 21:25, gives a sad summary of this book: "In those days Israel had no king; everyone did as he saw fit."

- What happens to a group of people with no leader or a weak leader?
- Does that sound like contemporary philosophy?
- Do you think people tend to draw closer to God or think more spiritually after a major catastrophe and then fall away again when times are better?

Ruth: The sweet story of the young woman named Ruth tells of her faith in the God of her mother-in-law, Naomi. Naomi helped Ruth "date" and then she won the heart of Boaz, a most eligible bachelor. Ruth later married Boaz. He became the father of Obed, the grandfather of Jesse, and the great grandfather of King David. This placed Ruth in the ancestral line of Christ.

1 Samuel: This begins the five hundred-year period of the kings of Israel. In 1 Samuel the Israelites asked God for a king like the other nations had. God was not pleased but granted their request and gave them Saul. The book of 1 Samuel covers a period of about 115 years. It begins with the childhood of Samuel and runs through Saul's kingship and then into the beginning of the reign of King David. Samuel was the last of the judges, and Saul was the first of the kings. Second Samuel tells us how David became Saul's successor on the throne. David was a mighty warrior and a wise king. The kingdom was expanded, and the nation was highly unified under David's rule.

Why do you think it displeased God so much when the Israelites insisted on having a king?

1 Kings: At King David's death, we see his son Solomon rise to the throne. He built the first temple, which was a large, elaborately decorated building. He had very specific building instructions from God (1 Kings 6). Solomon was known for his wisdom, but later in his life, he sought poor advice from friends and did not listen to God. His choice to do this actually changed the history of Israel. After his death, the kingdom divided under two leaders, Jeroboam and Rehoboam. It split into the northern kingdom, or Israel, and the southern kingdom, or Judah. II Kings gives us some of the history of the different kings of the two kingdoms. The southern kingdom (Judah) had twenty kings, and the northern kingdom (Israel) had nineteen kings. Some of Judah's leaders were godly and some wicked. All of the kings of Israel were wicked; none led their subjects to worship the true God. Henrietta Mears said, "During Solomon's reign the kingdom reached the height of its grandeur. With the death of Solomon, the kingship really ceased to be the medium through which God governed His people. The decline of the kingdoms is portrayed until we see both Israel and Judah led into captivity." Henrietta Mears, *What the Bible is All About* (Venture, CA: Regal Books, 1983) p 136. The Assyrians captured the Northern Kingdom in 722 BC, and the Southern Kingdom fell to the Babylonians around 586 BC.

In 1 Kings 2:1-4, David is about to die and gives a charge to his son. This is advice he wants his son to remember. What did David say?

Song of the week: "You Reign" by Mercy Me

LESSON 4

Synopsis of the Bible, Part III
I Chronicles Through Song of Solomon

1 Chronicles: This book gives us some history parallel to that of II Samuel. It begins with the death of Saul, gives many details about the reign of David, and ends with David's death.
II Chronicles parallels 1 Kings, with Solomon's reign and the division of the kingdom. It goes further to tell about the succeeding kings in both Israel and Judah.

Both the Assyrians and Babylonians carried Israelites away captive. The captives from Israel never returned from exile in Assyria. Some of the captives from Judah did return from exile in Babylon to rebuild the temple, its walls, and the city of Jerusalem, which had been destroyed by the Babylonians.

Ezra and Nehemiah: These two books tell of the return of the captives and the restoration of the temple and Jerusalem under the rule of the Persians who conquered the Babylonians. The time covered by these two books is approximately a hundred years.

What if your home land was destroyed by war or a natural disaster? Do you think you would return to repair and rebuild?

Esther: In 479 BC Esther became the queen of Persia when she became the wife of Xerxes. God placed Esther in the palace to preserve the Jewish nation from extinction. God had great plans for his chosen people. He intended to bless the whole world through them, and he did so by sending the Messiah and giving the world the Scriptures and the belief in one God through the Jews.

Just like there was a special God-appointed time, place, and purpose for Esther in history, there is also one for you!

The Poetry Books
Job, Psalms, Proverbs, Ecclesiastes, and Song of Solomon

Job: This is considered the oldest book of the Bible, and it deals with one of the oldest problems: why do bad things happen to good people? People have always been perplexed and frustrated when God permits his faithful to suffer. This book takes you through many stages of Job's suffering. Think of how faithful Job was to God. He did not have Scripture to guide him, yet he offered sacrifices to God on behalf of his children. He also remained faithful through his bodily suffering and the rejection of God by his wife and friends!

God uses trials and suffering in our lives many different ways. Can you think of some? Would anyone like to share a personal example?

Psalms: The Hebrew title of Psalms is "Praise" or the "Book of Praises," and the main content of this book is praise, prayer, and worship. The Psalms were like the national hymnal of Israel. They contain 150 poems to be sung to music. These poems run through a full range of human emotion: joy, sorrow, victory, failure, trust, fear, and pleas for help. Each scripture should be considered with its context.

Proverbs: Here we find wise counsel for everyday living.

There are thirty-one chapters in Proverbs. This book makes a wonderful daily devotional since there is one chapter for each day of the month.

Ecclesiastes: Solomon tells of his search for meaning, purpose, and happiness in life. He tried it all, saying that everything but *knowing God* is a dead end. It's useless, meaningless, and could be considered vanity in the long run. He gives his conclusion in Ecclesiastes 12:13: "Fear God, and keep his commandments: for this is the whole duty of man."

What are some things people use today to fill their lives with happiness and meaning? Do these things truly fulfill? For how long?

Song of Solomon: The Song of Solomon has been called the Christian's love song. The love between a man and a woman in this book gives us a picture of the love between God and his people. The greatest commandment is for us to love God with all our heart, soul, mind, and strength. We are challenged to such wholehearted devotion in the Song of Solomon.

Today's study has given us another history lesson but also introduced us to the beautiful poetry books. They encourage us during our suffering and help us overcome adversity. They give us hymns of praise and verses of wise counsel. Man has always searched for the meaning of life, and I love the way Solomon puts it—everything but knowing God is useless!

Song of the Week: "Word of God Speak" by Mercy Me

LESSON 5

Synopsis of the Bible, Part IV
The Books of Prophecy and the New Testament

This is the final lesson in our walk through the Bible. Hopefully it will give you an overall view of what the Bible encompasses.

The seventeen prophetic books in the Old Testament are divided into two categories: the Major Prophets, of which there are five; and the Minor Prophets, of which there are twelve. The messages of the Minor Prophets are not necessarily less important than the messages of the Major Prophets, but the books are shorter!

Remember how faithful and caring God has been to his people. He led them out of captivity and through the Red Sea. He gave them the Ten Commandments to guide them. Instead of reverencing and obeying God, the Israelite people chose to do their own thing and not listen to God's instructions. At this time, God raised up prophets to lead the people. These prophets spoke courageously to kings and common people alike. They not only addressed sins and failures but also gave promises of God's comfort.

Who today would you liken to the Old Testament prophets?

Let's take a look at *Daniel*, one of the more familiar prophets. Read Daniel 9 to see an example of a prophet's job.

After the last voice of the prophets died out, there were four hundred years of silence from God to man before the birth of Jesus. In other words, there were four hundred years between the Old and New Testaments.

Remember the Northern Kingdom, or Israel, was conquered by the Assyrians around 722 BC, and many of the people were carried into exile. The Southern Kingdom, or Judah, was conquered by the Babylonians around 586 BC, and many of the Jews were taken into exile.

The prophets can be divided into those who prophesied to Israel and those who prophesied to Judah. They can also be divided into those who prophesied before part of the Jewish nation was taken captive into exile, those who prophesied during the exile, and those who prophesied after the exile.

The prophets to Israel before their exile were Jonah, Amos, and Hosea. The prophets to Judah before their exile were Obadiah, Joel, Isaiah, Micah, Nahum, Habakkuk, Zephaniah, and Jeremiah.

The prophets during the exile or captivity in Babylon were Ezekiel and Daniel. Jeremiah extended partially into this period as well.

Those who prophesied to Judah after the exile were Haggai, Zechariah, and Malachi.

Prophets were never sent when a nation was walking in obedience to God. They were always sent to warn the people that God was displeased with them and tell them what would happen if they continued down the wrong road. Not only did the prophets speak of judgment to come, but they often foretold future events as well.

New Testament

God loved his children so much that he went to all kinds of measures to communicate with them. How would you have communicated if there were no phones, computers, or TVs? You might have written a letter. God wrote us a beautiful love letter. It is the Bible. He communicated through prophets, angels, burning bushes, dreams, and natural phenomena. Now he is about to make the boldest move of all. He is actually coming to earth to try to woo us to himself in person! He is a pursuer God.

The Gospels
Matthew, Mark, Luke, and John

These are actual first-hand accounts from men who walked and talked with Jesus. They were from different walks of life. Matthew was a tax collector. Mark's occupation was not given. Luke was a doctor. John was a fisherman. They all had very different backgrounds and education. This made their accounts of the same event unique.

Matthew: Was written primarily to the Jews and contains a number of Scriptures that show how Jesus fulfilled some of the Old Testament prophecies.

Mark: Was written primarily for the Romans, who were men of action. It is fast moving and tells more of what Jesus did than what he said.

Luke: Was primarily written to the Gentiles. It has a more universal appeal.

John: Was written so that whoever reads this book may conclude that Jesus is the Christ, the Son of God. John concentrated on Jesus' miracles and explained the meanings behind them.

The remainder of the New Testament contains the following:

Acts: A history book. This book tells of Pentecost and the early days of the church.

Romans, 1 & 2 Corinthians, Galatians, Ephesians, Philippians, Colossians, 1 & 2 Thessalonians, 1 & 2 Timothy, Titus, Philemon, Hebrews, James, 1 & 2 Peter, 1, 2 & 3 John, and Jude: These books include twenty-one epistles (letters), fourteen of which were written by Paul. Many were written to instruct and encourage the new churches that were started as a result of the impact that Jesus' life had upon the earth.

Revelation: The book of the future. This book is John's "vision into heaven." It is a prophetic view of what is to come. God and Satan will have their last "showdown." One day Christ will return to gather his believers. Some refer to this as the rapture. After Christ's return, the Bible tells us that there will be a time of tremendous suffering for the people left on earth. Those who are unbelievers will have a time period to turn to the Lord and be saved. Revelation also gives us a glimpse of all the wonderful things that await believers in heaven. At this time, read Revelation 22.

- The Old Testament tells us to "get ready" because someone is coming.
- The Gospels tell us, "He is here."
- Revelation tells us, "He is coming again."

The book of Revelation tells us that Jesus Christ will one day return as King of kings and Lord of lords to reign forever. He is coming back to receive his church. Won't it be exciting to be a part of his story!

Song of the Week: "When the Saints Go Marching In" by Sara Groves

LESSON 6

How Do We Know That the Bible Is Really God's Word?

Do you believe that the Bible is true? Is it trustworthy? Is it believable?

We have already seen that the Bible is a unique book. No other book could possess the characteristics and the history that the Bible contains without having been written by the hand of God. Think about it . . .

The Bible is unique in its *continuity*. We learned that the Bible was written over a time span of fourteen hundred to sixteen hundred years by approximately forty authors from many different walks of life. It was written on three continents and in three languages, yet there is harmony and agreement throughout. The Bible tells one story from beginning to end.

The Bible is unique in its *circulation*. It is, far and away, the best seller of all time. No other book has approached its number of copies—printed or read.

The Bible is unique in its *survival*. It has survived being tediously copied by hand many times with remarkable accuracy. It has also survived criticism, skepticism, and persecution.

The Bible is more than just *unique*. It claims to be written by God himself.

Look up these Scriptures:

- 2 Peter 1:20-21:

- 2 Timothy 3:16:

In the production of Scripture, both God and man were active participants. God worked through human authors to give us his words. The writings were colored by the unique personalities and circumstances of each individual writer, but God caused each one to write what he wanted. This is what is meant when you hear that Scripture is the *inspired* Word of God.

A. The Old Testament asserts that its writings are from God. Over two thousand examples are found and the following are just a few:

- Isaiah 1:2b:
- Ezekiel 6:1:
- Hosea 4:1:
- Amos 1:3:

B. New Testament writers believed that their words were inspired by God as well. Paul wrote to the Thessalonians, "And we also thank God continually because, when you received the word of God, which you heard from us, you accepted it not as the word of men, but as it actually is, the word of God, which is at work in you who believe" (I Thessalonians 2:13).

Paul also wrote in I Corinthians 2:13:

C. Jesus recognized the Old Testament as being from God and quoted it on numerous occasions. Matthew 5:17-18, Deuteronomy 8:3, Matthew 19:4-5.

Jesus believed that the entire Old Testament was the Word of God. If we believe Jesus, we will believe the Bible. Further, if we believe the Bible, we should believe Jesus. This belief is fundamental to the doctrine of the Christian faith.

How can we understand the Bible? The Holy Spirit is the one who guides us in understanding and applying God's Word. I Corinthians 2:11-12 says, "For who among men knows the thoughts of a man except the man's spirit within him? In the same way no one knows the thoughts of God except the Spirit of God. We have not received the spirit of the world but the Spirit who is from God, that we may understand what God has freely given us."

Who has the Holy Spirit living in them to give this understanding? It is the people who acknowledge that they are sinners and cannot do anything to make themselves pure before a Holy God. They accept that Jesus Christ has died on the cross to pay the penalty for their sins. They receive God's complete forgiveness and now have Jesus' righteousness imputed to them. (In other words, when God looks at them, he sees people with a clean record!) They are now beloved, adopted children of God. They are filled with the Holy Spirit who will never, ever leave them!

Do you believe that all Scripture is true for all people all of the time? For example:
1) Is it okay to be dishonest sometimes?
2) Is it okay to cheat on a test if everyone is doing it?
3) Is it okay to make fun of your mother to your friends?
4) Is it okay to use God's name without respect?

How about stealing, jealousy, and adultery?

There are two ways to look at the world: a biblical way and a non-biblical way.

Proverbs 14:12:

Many people want to live in a way that seems right to *them,* not by the teachings of the *Bible.* Many will argue that we should be "tolerant" of other people's beliefs and claim that what is right or wrong for you might not be right or wrong for me.

There is a body of absolute truth, truth that is true in every situation, and this body of truth is found in the Bible. Scripture gives us the truth about God, about creation including mankind, about sin and salvation, and about the eternal future of each person.

I love the fact that the same Ten Commandments that God gave to Moses some thirty-five hundred years ago are still relevant today. The sinful heart of man is basically facing the same old problems that it faced in biblical times and has dealt with ever since.

The Ten Commandments
Exodus 20

1) I am the Lord your God. You shall have no other God's before me.

2) You shall not make for yourself an idol.

3) You shall not misuse the name of the Lord your God.

4) Remember the Sabbath day by keeping it holy.

5) Honor your father and your mother.

6) You shall not murder.

7) You shall not commit adultery.

8) You shall not steal.

9) You shall not give false testimony.

10) You shall not covet.

What do you notice about the ordering of the commandments?

Only God could provide us with these "living" rules that have instructed the action and touched the heart of man for centuries. Take the time to memorize these to use as a guide for yourself and also as a wonderful tool for sharing with others.

Song of the week: "The Word" by Sara Groves

LESSON 7

How Was the Bible Made, and How Do We Know it is Reliable?

The Bible is a story of dedication to painstaking detail. How often do we neglect to recognize and remember the thousands of years of sacrificial effort that went into the Bible that we so easily take for granted today?

A. Jewish scholars, called Talmudists, were designated to copy the Scriptures. The copyist had to wash his whole body and sit in full Jewish dress to copy a manuscript.

B. A synagogue roll had to be written on the skins of clean animals that had been prepared for the special task.

C. The ink was to be black only and prepared by a particular recipe.

D. The transcriber had to copy from an authenticated manuscript and was not to deviate in the least.

E. No word or letter, not even a yod (punctuation mark), was to be written from memory, but the scribe had to look at each one individually as he copied.

F. Between every consonant, there had to be the space of a hair or a thread. Between every new section, there had to be the breadth of nine consonants. Between every book, there was to be the space of three lines.

G. The copyists were so particular with the manuscripts that they counted the number of verses, the number of words, and the number of letters in each book. They found the middle letter of each page and each book. They even knew the middle letter of the Pentateuch and of the whole Old Testament. They carefully checked all copies by comparing the numbers of verses, words, and letters and the middle letters to see if they all matched.

Old Testament

The Pentateuch (the first five books in the Bible) is called the Law of Moses. Jesus referred to these books as being authored by Moses. How could Moses have known about the creation of the world?

1. God could have supernaturally given Moses this information, or
2. This information could have been passed down orally from generation to generation until people began to write things down.

Have you asked your parents to tell you stories? Did you have your favorites that you wanted to hear over and over again?

There was written language before Moses lived, so there could have been some written accounts of creation. Before written language, there were cave drawings. Moses could have had access to both written and oral accounts of the creation when he wrote Genesis.

What are some of the ways the Old Testament books might have been given by God to be written and preserved?

1) Moses _____ what God told him to.
2) God spoke to and _____ who preceded their writings with such sayings as, "Thus saith the Lord."
3) Some of the books tell the story of the events of the Jews. They are _____
   _____.
4) The _____ were the hymns of the Jewish nation.

Jesus himself referred to the Old Testament *canon* in Luke 24:44 when he told the disciples in the upper room, "Everything must be fulfilled, that is written about me in the Law of Moses, the Prophets and the Psalms." These were the three sections in which the Hebrew Bible was divided. Jesus quoted or made reference to thirty-five Old Testament books, confirming that he accepted them.

Look up and write the meaning of the word "canon."

What are the books of the *Apocrypha?*

The Apocrypha are books included in the Septuagint and Vulgate but excluded from the Jewish and Protestant canons of the Old Testament, or early Christian writings not included in the New Testament.

Many other spiritual writings appeared on the scene. The Jews were careful to define which books would be included in the canon, the accepted Word of God.

New Testament

The acceptance of the books of the New Testament was a little different from the books of the Old Testament. The first-century Christians actually recorded the words of Jesus and of the apostles. The New Testament books were either written by eyewitnesses to Jesus' ministry or by those who heard firsthand these eyewitness reports.

Canonicity is *determined or fixed* by God; it is merely *discovered* by man. There were several guidelines for including a book in the New Testament canon.

1) Were the writers reliable? Was a book written by an apostle or someone who knew an apostle well and had heard him speak often?
2) Was the content reliable? Did it agree with the rest of Scripture? Did it have a sense of divine authority?
3) Was it read and used by the people of God? The accepted books were circulated through the churches and read publicly.
4) How did the early church fathers regard these books?

Josephus, the Jewish historian, wrote this at the end of the first century AD: "And how firmly we have given credit to those books of our own nation is evident by what we do: for during so many ages as have already passed, no one has been so bold as either to add anything to them or take anything from them or to make any change in them: but it becomes natural to all Jews, immediately and from their very birth, to esteem those books to contain divine doctrines, and to persist in time, and, if occasion be, willingly to die for them." Flavius Josephus, "Flavius Josephus Against Apion." *Josephus, Complete Works.* Translated by William Whiston, Grand Rapids, OR: Kregel Publications, 1960) p 609.

Athanasius of Alexandria (AD 367) gives us the earliest list of New Testament books that is exactly like our present New Testament in a letter to the churches.

F. F. Bruce states, "When at last a Church Council—the Synod of Hippo in A.D. 393—listed the 27 books of the New Testament, it did not confer upon them any authority which they did not already possess, but simply recorded their previously established canonicity." F.F. Bruce, *The Books and the Parchments*, Rev. ed. (Westwood, NJ: Fleming H. Revell Co., 1963) p 97.

Josh McDowell concludes, "Since this time, there has been no serious questioning of the 27 accepted books of the New Testament." Josh McDowell, *Evidence that Demands a Verdict* (San Bernardino, CA: Here's Life Publishers, Inc., 1972, 1979) p 38.

You can imagine how scarce and expensive copies of the Bible before the invention of the printing press would be. Very few people had Bibles in their homes. How many Bibles would you estimate you have in your home? Do you realize what a privilege it is to have instant access to the very Word of God? Are we taking full advantage of this opportunity?

A wonderful way to prove the authenticity of the Bible is to study the prophecies that were predicted and study the way in which they were fulfilled. Fulfilled prophecy is one way to see God's absolute authority and understand he is in control over the actions of heaven and earth.

What are some different methods used today to predict what is going to happen in the future?

How accurate are their outcomes?

The test of a true biblical prophet is that **all** of his predictions have to come true! He must be 100 percent correct to be a true prophet of God. In other words, there must be divine guidance and no room for human error.

The Bible contains hundreds of detailed prophecies which have been fulfilled.

You can be confident when you read your Bible that is the inspired Word of God. It has been proven over and over, not only by fulfilled prophesies, but also by its ability to change men's hearts. I Thessalonians 2:13 says it best: "And we also thank God continually because, when you received the word of God, which you heard from us, you accepted it not as the word of men, but as it actually is, the word of God, which is at work in you who believe."

Song of the Week: "Thy Word" by Amy Grant

LESSON 8

JESUS, THE CENTERPIECE OF THE WORD

Suppose a man were to walk in here right now and claim to be God in human form. Would you believe him? Don't you think we would ask him for proof? After all, in this era of identity theft, our credentials that prove who we are have become very important, and we are required to tell or show them on certain occasions.

What are some credentials that can be shown to prove who you are?

When God sent Jesus into the world, he knew people would be very skeptical. After all, nothing like this had ever happened before. He wanted people to recognize Jesus as who he really was, God in the flesh, so God gave Jesus some important credentials that would authenticate his claim. Think about it—if God became man, what credentials do you think he should have? What would we expect him to be like?

If *God became a man,* we would expect his birth to be different. Jesus' birth was unusual. What was "not the norm" concerning Jesus' birth?

If *God became a man,* we would expect him to be without sin, to be morally perfect.

What did Pilate say about Jesus at his trial? Luke 23:4

Read Matthew 27:3-5. What did Judas say about Jesus?

Read 1 Peter 2:22. Peter said,

When Jesus asked his enemies what sin he had committed, they were unable to name a single one.

If *God became a man,* we would expect him to have an acute sense of his difference from others.

25

Remember the twelve-year-old boy Jesus when he accompanied his parents to the temple in Jerusalem and stayed behind? When his parents questioned him, Jesus said, "Didn't you know I had to be in my Father's house?" Luke 2:49.

Jesus claimed to be God a number of times and in different ways.

1) Matthew 26:53

2) John 14:9

Jesus claimed to forgive sins, a privilege of God alone. Jesus claimed to be the judge of all men. Jesus asked men to put their eternal destiny in his hands. In Luke 23:47, the centurion

Jesus very clearly claimed to be deity. Mark 14:61b-62

Jesus made his claims so clear that his enemies understood them.

How did his enemies react to his claims?

John 5:18

John 10:36

If *God became a man,* we would expect other people to recognize him as divine.

In John 1:45, Philip declared,

In John 1:49, Nathanael said to Jesus,

In John 11:27, Martha answered,

And when Thomas saw Jesus for himself after the resurrection, he called Jesus, "my Lord and my God." John 20:28

These people knew Jesus well. But maybe Jesus' friends were prejudiced. What did others say about him?

In Luke 23:41, the repentant thief on the cross said,

In Luke 23:47, the centurion who was in charge of the crucifixion said,

If *God became man,* we would expect him to perform miracles, and Jesus certainly did that.

If *God became man,* we would expect him to speak the greatest words ever spoken.

Luke 4:22

John 7:46

In John 6:68, Simon Peter answered him,

If *God became man,* we would surely expect him to have a lasting influence on mankind.

From the essay entitled "One Solitary Life," we find these words, "Nineteen long centuries have come and gone, and today He is the centerpiece of the human race and the leader of the column of progress. I am far within the mark when I say that all the armies that ever marched, all the navies that ever were built, all the parliaments that ever sat, and all the kings that ever reigned, put together, have not affected the life of man upon this earth as powerfully as has that one solitary life." Dr. James Allan Francis, "Arise Sir Knight!" *The Real Jesus and Other Sermons* (Philadelphia, PA: The Judson Press of Philadelphia, 1926) pp 123-124.

Many still do not want to acknowledge Jesus as the Son of God, the Messiah, and the Savior of the World. They will say he was just a "good man" or a "great teacher." This is not possible because he claimed to be the Son of God. If he was just a good man or a great teacher, he would now be a liar because he said on many occasions that he was God's son. There was no room for compromise.

Song of the week: "Above All" by Michael W. Smith

PART TWO

The Bible, What Does It Mean to Me?

LESSON 9

MY PERSONAL JOURNEY OF FAITH

We have spent the past eight lessons examining the authorship, structure, and authenticity of the Bible. Now it is time for application. What significance does all of this have for you personally?

Before we see where this information will lead you, let's see where you have been. Where did your spiritual journey begin? What has helped shape your faith? You are all probably at different levels of spiritual maturity. No doubt some of you are very devoted to your heavenly father and are walking closely day by day. Others may still have many questions. Some of you may not have made a commitment to God at all.

Much of the Bible is devoted to genealogy. Let's take a look and see where some of your heritage lies. Fill in the names and give one or two traits for each person on your family tree.

YOUR NAME

FATHER

MOTHER

FATHER'S PARENTS

MOTHER'S PARENTS

Like it or not, not only is eye color passed down through family lines. More times than not, actions can be passed down as well. The Bible confirms this:

- Nehemiah 1:6b

- Nehemiah 9:2

- Ezekiel 18:14

- Psalm 79:8

- Jeremiah 32:18a

Good and bad traits are passed down from grandparents and parents to their children. For example, it has been noted that many times when people are abused, they often later become abusers.

If you have had some "undesirable traits" passed down to you, don't despair. God is in the life changing business. The chain *can* be broken! One reason you are here is to learn and apply the attributes of Godly behavior.

Spiritual Training

Record church affiliations, Sunday school, VBS, and other spiritual training you have had.

_____

_____

Record the names of people who have had a positive impact on your life.

_____

_____

Record a favorite childhood memory.

_____

_____

Read Psalm 139:13-18. God knew the day you were born, just as he knows exactly when he will call you to your heavenly home. Your childhood is no surprise to him. He can use the good and the bad events of your past. He never wastes an opportunity to help you grow!

Take this time to write a letter to God. Just be honest with him; he already knows your heart. You might want to thank him for your family history, the good and the bad. You might want to thank him for the opportunities he has presented to you. You might ask for his wisdom and guidance in studying his Word and tell him of your desire to know him more!

Look on the internet for popular Christian author, Josh McDowell, and read his testimony.

Song of the week: "My Life Is in Your Hands" by Kirk Franklin

LESSON 10

Early Examples of Faith

In our last lesson, we talked about different traits we have—good and bad, inherited and learned. You wrote a letter to God expressing your desire to know him more. Do you really believe that "his ways" will make your life better, more fulfilled, and successful? Remember the Israelites? When they did things God's way, there was no need for prophets to intervene, but when they sinned, they suffered the consequences.

Since we cannot see God with our eyes at this time, we must believe or have faith with our minds and hearts. That is what today's lesson is about.

A good starting point would be Hebrews 11, also known as the faith chapter.

1. Hebrews 11:1 gives us a definition of *faith*. The Living Bible, Tyndale Publishing, translates like this: "It is the confident assurance that something we want is going to happen. It is the certainty that what we hope for is waiting for us, even though we cannot see it up ahead."

2. What do the words confident, assurance, and certainty convey to you?

3. What evidence of God does Hebrew 11:3 reveal?

    Psalm 19:1-4 expands on this. Read it.

4. Do "all men, women, and children for all times" have access to this evidence?

In Hebrews 11:4 we see the beginning of the "roll call" of the faithful.

5. Who is the first person mentioned in Hebrews 11:4?

6. In verse 5, what amazing reward did Enoch receive for his faithfulness?

7. Verse 6 shares a very important truth with us. What is it?

8. Who are the faithful mentioned in verses 7 through 12, and how did they demonstrate their faith?

9. Verses 13 through 16 reveal something about the people of faith previously mentioned. What is it?

How is a life different when a person lives for the hope of heaven instead of the things this world has to offer?

10. In verses 17 through 19, we see the story of Abraham and his son Isaac. This is one of the most incredible stories of faith ever written. Read and discuss.

God wants us to "lay our Isaacs" on the altar. Our Isaac is anything that we love more than we love God. Sometimes God requires a sacrifice from us, and sometimes he just wants to know if we are willing to make the sacrifice.

11. Verse 23 tells us that Moses' parents had faith as well. How did they act on it?

Verses 23 through 32 tell of Moses and others who did great things because of their faith.

Do good things always happen to faithful people? Does God always reward our faith with what we want?

At this point, I want you to read the rest of the faith chapter and discuss what is happening. Does the different treatment seem fair to us?

Verses 39 and 40 tell us that sometimes God wants us to wait and share the even better rewards that were prepared for us.

Song of the week: "He's Always Been Faithful" by Sara Groves

LESSON 11

LORD, I WANT TO KNOW YOU MORE!

The entire Bible shows us God's efforts to know and fellowship with us. He talked to Adam in the garden. He gave us his incredible creation to see his handiwork. He sent prophets, allowed kings, sent judges, arranged angelic visits, and finally came to earth himself. Knowing God and desiring his ways will have a profound impact on your life!

Galatians 5:16-24—the Fruit of the Spirit

1. We need to walk in the _____, not in the _____.
2. The flesh and the spirit are _____ to one another.
3. The deeds of the flesh are:

4. What is the result of practicing the deeds of the flesh (v. 21)?

    Read Psalm 1:1-3
5. The man who delights in the Lord will produce much what? _____
6. Galatians 5:22-23 tells us what the fruits of the spirit are. List them.

What can you do to make sure you are a "fruit bearer"?
Galatians 5:25

Spiritual breathing—Just as we exhale carbon dioxide, we spiritually exhale the sin in our lives by confessing it. Just as we breathe in oxygen, we ask God's spirit to fill and control our lives once again. (This concept was taken from Dr. Bill Bright of Campus Crusade International.)

Hang out with the right people!

Fill up with God's goodness. Like the tree by the river, drink it in at every opportunity.

Song of the Week: "Oh, I Want to Know You More"

LESSON 12

ARMOR OF GOD

"Put on the full armor of God so that you can take your stand against the devil's schemes."
Ephesians 6:11

Read Ephesians 6:10-17.

1. What is armor used for, and why would Paul use this metaphor to help us "arm" ourselves as Christians? (Verse 10 gives a clue.)

2. What are the "wiles of the devil"? (See 2 Corinthians 11:3)

3. In Ephesians 6:12, we learn that our battle is not with humans but with whom?

4. What do you make of Ephesians 6:13-14a?

    We need to be prepared *ahead of time.* Evil will come our way!

5. Listed below are the six pieces of armor mentioned. What does each of these represent?

-   Belt

-   Breastplate

-   Feet

- Shield

- Helmet

- Sword

Notice the Christian does not have anything to protect his back. We are not supposed to retreat; we are to stand firm!

Art Project

Song of the Week: "Armor of God" by Patrick Ryan Clark

LESSON 13

DO I HAVE MY HELMET ON?

"For God so loved the world that he gave his one and only Son, that whoever believes in him shall not perish but have eternal life." John 3:16

In the last lesson we talked about putting on all of God's armor so that we could stand against the ways of Satan. This week we will talk about the crucial piece of armor that commits you to the family of God for eternity.

1. Ephesians 6:17 tells us that we are to take on the "helmet of *salvation.*" What do you think this could mean?

2. Look up the word "salvation" in the dictionary and record the meaning here.

3. What do we, as humans, need to be saved from? Romans 3:23

God created us for his pleasure, to walk with him in the garden and to be companions for him. We, like Adam and Eve, from time to time, follow our own sinful desires and break off companionship with him. He is a holy God and can have no fellowship with our rebellious life of sin.

4. Romans 6:23

Remember the different sacrifices that Cain and Abel offered to God for their sins? Remember the strict laws of the Old Testament and the animal sacrifices? Remember the priests and judges whose jobs were to point out and help people deal with their sins?

In the New Testament God reveals the provision he has made for us to deal with our sin problem *directly.* It is through the sacrifice and the shedding of his son's blood.

5. Romans 5:8

John 14:6

Romans 8:1a

In other words, we are sinful and cannot approach God. He has made a way for us to have fellowship with him by offering his son. Why he chose to do it this way is a mystery to us, but he is God. His ways are not our ways; they are higher and better. There is something that we must do individually with his wonderful provision!

6. John 1:12

*Is this **all** that God **requires** of us? (Surely we must be missionaries, sing in the choir, give to the poor, and never cuss or fuss!)*

7. Ephesians 2:8-9

He desires a relationship with *you!* It is a *free* gift, *you don't* have to work for it—only believe and receive it. Honestly, is there *anything* that we could do that would ever merit this wonderful gift?

8. Revelation 3:20

If you have never invited Christ into your life, this would be a good time. His desire is that none should perish but all experience *his abundant* life and have everlasting life with him. You may do so by praying and asking forgiveness for your sins and by telling God you appreciate him sending his son to make a provision for the forgiveness of your sins. By doing so, you are telling God that you would like him to take and control your life and produce the kind of fruit in you that comes from knowing and following him.

Prayer Opportunity

9. Did you ask God into your life? According to Revelation 3:20, where is he?

10. What wonderful promise do we find in Hebrew 13:5?

Congratulations if you prayed this prayer today for the first time! You are a new baby in the family of God. It is great that you are in a Bible study so you can grow and learn from his Word. For those of you who have already accepted Christ as your Savior, I pray that you are growing in your walk with God. What advice would you give a new Christian?

What if you sometimes have doubts that you might not be a Christian sometime? Where do you think that kind of thinking comes from? What does the Bible (the eternal Word of God) tell you? Hebrews 13:5 says *He will never leave you!*

Song of the week: "Give Me Your Eyes" by Brandon Heath

LESSON 14

Empty Me So I Can Be Filled with You

Once you have made a decision to "believe and receive" what should you do next?

Paul is writing to the new church in Philippi. Philippians 2:3-15 says:

Do nothing out of _____ or _____, but in _____ consider others better than yourselves. Each of you should look not only to your own interests, but also to the interests of _____. Your attitude should be the same as that of Christ Jesus: Who, being in very nature God, did not consider _____ with God something to be grasped, but made himself _____, taking the very nature of a _____, being made in human likeness. And being found in appearance as a _____, he humbled himself and became _____to death—even death on a cross! Therefore God exalted him to the highest place and gave him the name that is above every name, that at the name of Jesus every _____, in heaven and on earth and under the earth, and every tongue confess that Jesus Christ is Lord, to the glory of God the Father. Therefore, my dear friends, as you have always _____—not only in my presence, but now much more in my absence—continue to work out your salvation with fear and trembling, for it is God who works in you to will and to act according to his good _____. Do everything without _____and _____,so that you may become _____ and _____, children of God without fault in a _____ and _____ generation, in which you shine like _____ in the universe.

The words "made himself nothing" are translated "made himself empty." Just as Christ emptied himself on the cross, so must we empty ourselves of sin, selfishness, pride, arrogance, and seeking our will before his. God didn't have to become a man. The man

Christ didn't have to become a servant. The servant man did not have to die for us. The death didn't have to be a cruel one on a cross.

He is *our* example of a Christian life. God allowed Christ to become a man to *identify* with us!

1. What was Christ's attitude toward others while he hung on the cross?

   - John 19:26-27 (concerning his mother)

   - Luke 23:34 (concerning those crucifying him)

   - Luke 23:40-43 (concerning the criminal being crucified with him)

2. How can you empty yourself of *you* to make room for *God's* agenda? It must be a conscious effort!

3. From the Philippians Scripture, list as many things as you can find from which you desire to be emptied.

4. What was Christ's attitude, and how could it help you to follow his example?

5. Who can you think of that could benefit from your obedience to Christ?

6. How can you shine like a star in a crooked and depraved world?

Anyway

Author Unknown

People are unreasonable, illogical and self-centered. Love them *anyway.*
If you do good, people will accuse you of selfish motives. Do good *anyway.*
The kindness you show today may be forgotten tomorrow. Be kind *anyway.*
What you spend years building may be destroyed overnight. Build *anyway.*
People really need help but may attack you if you help them. Help them *anyway.*
Give the world the best you've got and you might get kicked in the teeth.
Give the best you've got *anyway.*

Don't you want to empty yourself to make room for what God can do in your life? Don't you want to *shine* for him?

Song of the week: "Empty Me" by Chris Sligh

LESSON 15

TAMING THE TONGUE

"Do not merely listen to the word, and so deceive yourselves. Do what it says."
James 1:22

One of the words you hear a lot of teenagers use today is *drama*. Drama can be used to describe actions, of course, but it can start and also manifest itself in speech. Let's face it, girls like to talk, and sometimes that talk can lead to *gossip*. What would you consider to be "gossip"?

There is an old saying, "Sticks and stones can break my bones but words will never hurt me." Do you think this is true? How does it make you feel when someone has spread something about you that is not true? Can it ruin your friendship?

Read James 3:3-4. What two things does James compare the tongue to?

These two small items have a huge impact on their subject. Get the picture! Read James 3:5-6. These verses even take things a step further. What power does the tongue have in this illustration?

Remember what Smokey the Bear says: "Only *you* can prevent *forest fires.*"

Have you ever had that "uh oh" feeling right before you said something that you shouldn't? I believe it is the Holy Spirit's guidance, a clear warning that you should just clam up! After you clam up, think: (Psalm 19:14)

Remember, one of our fruits of the spirit is self-control. What do I Peter 3:10, Proverbs 15:28, and Proverbs 16:23 suggest?

- I Peter 3:10

- Proverbs 15:28:

- Proverbs 16:23:

Even better, let's use our speech for building our friends up! What does a trustworthy friend do? Proverbs 11:13

I'm sure you've all had the experience when someone said a kind word at just the right time. It can mean the world to you. You might have just been sitting in the cafeteria alone and a friend invited you to join her at the table. It's great to feel accepted. The Bible says that a word spoken in the right circumstances is like: (Proverbs 25:11)

Edwin Markham (1852-1940) wrote a little poem that went like this:

> He drew a circle that shut me out—
> Heretic, rebel, a thing to flout.
> But love and I had the wit to win,
> We drew a circle that took him in!

Read Proverbs 17:17. It tells us that a true friend loves when?

We all mess up from time to time. If you don't listen to the "uh oh" call of the spirit and go ahead and share something about a friend that you shouldn't, what should you do to make things right with that person and with God?

Thought: While chatting with your fingers when you are texting, on Twitter, e-mailing, and on Facebook, think long and hard before you hit the send button. Don't send something that you wouldn't want anybody else to read or that you will regret later!

Song of the week: "Do Everything" by Steven Curtis Chapman

LESSON 16

PRETTY IS AS PRETTY DOES

"Like a gold ring in a pig's snout is a beautiful woman who shows no discretion."
Proverbs 11:22

Describe a "lady" in your own words.

Describe a "woman worthy of praise" in your own words.

Can you think of any "worthy ladies" who would be good role models for young girls today?

Proverbs 31:30 says, "Charm is deceptive, and beauty is fleeting; but a woman who fears the Lord is to be praised." Discuss the meaning of this verse.

Proverbs 31:31 says, "Give her the reward she has earned, and let her works bring her praise at the city gate." Discuss the meaning of this verse.

You might say "her reputation precedes her." Have you ever heard the saying, "Reputations are like fine china, easily broken and hard to repair"?

What actions can bring a girl a good reputation (remember our fruits of the spirit)?

What actions do you think bring a girl a bad reputation?

Let's look back at Galatians 5:19-21. What actions does the Bible tell us to avoid?

What can you do to avoid these behaviors and their effects on your life?

An old expression says, "If you lie down with dogs you will get up with fleas." Proverbs 13:20 states it differently. Write out this verse and discuss.

Can you see how the friends you run with can greatly influence you?

While we like to blame our sinful actions on the influence of others, we alone are responsible for our actions. The world offers more impure opportunities than ever before, but the same temptations that are pulling on you have been around ever since the Garden of Eden. It is up to you to decide, "Am I going to follow the ways of the Lord or the deeds of the flesh?"

How can you ever begin to escape all the temptations that are surrounding you? The escape begins in your _____. Philippians 4:8 tells us to think about what?

Is this the way you naturally think? Of course not! You must decide that your desire is to follow God and that you want to please him. Romans 12:2 says that you must be "transformed by the renewing of your mind."

Below are four different areas in which teens will have to face decisions on how God would have them behave. Remember, pretty is as pretty does.

1) **Your Body and Appearance**

   I Corinthians 6:19-20

   All of these things fall into this category: skin care, weight, oral hygiene, sleep, drugs, smoking, posture and sitting, and "lazy language."

   What about your appearance? I Timothy 2:9-10

   Have you ever watched the TV show *What Not to Wear*? What does the way you dress say about you?

2) **How You Spend Your Time**

Are you preparing yourself for greatness or just biding your time? Do you study properly? Do you waste time in front of the TV? Are you thinking constantly about what would please you or are you considering the needs of others?

3) **How Do You Treat Your Parents?**

One of the Ten Commandments is Exodus 20:12 which states: "Honor your father and your mother, so that you may live long in the land the Lord your God is giving you."

Ephesians 6:1

Proverbs 5:20-23

4) **Dating (Next Lesson)**

Song of the week: "My Heart Your Home" by Christy Nockels

LESSON 17

Dating

"Don't let anyone look down on you because you are young, but set an example for the believers in speech, in life, in love, in faith and in purity." I Timothy 4:12

I chose a positive verse for this lesson because I think dating should be a positive and fun experience. Being noticed by boys and interacting with them is fun and exciting!
Tell me what the dating world is like today. Do you have an age limit for when you can single date? What are your some of your parents' rules about dating?

It is interesting to read stories of romantic encounters in the Bible. I can just picture Naomi getting Ruth all "gussied" up to go and meet Boaz and Esther putting on her royal robes and jewels to meet with King Ahasuerus and trying to persuade him to save her people. God has given you beauty and charms to attract the opposite sex. After all, God made boys so darn cute that we couldn't help but be attracted to them. Thank goodness he has also given us guidelines in his Word for a healthy dating experience. As a Christian, your dating life should be quite different from the swept away, instant romance, sexual episodes you see portrayed in movies, TV, and romance novels.

What insight does the Bible give us in this area? The Scriptures don't say a lot about the actual dating process, but they do assure you that God has a specific plan for your life (Jer. 29:11), and that we are to be careful about who we choose to date (II Cor. 6:14). There are also many Scriptures that warn us to stay sexually pure (II Tim. 2:22, 1 Cor. 6:18, 1 Thess. 4:3-5, Eph. 5:3).

1) How does the media today portray dating, romance and sex to the average teen?

As you can see, God's ideals are far different from the world's view, and the consequences from ignoring God can be heartbreaking. There is no other area in life that causes as many regrets as being sexually impure.

2) What are some of the regrets you might experience as a result of diving in too fast and too far with the opposite sex?

3) What happens to us when we don't heed God's advice in any area of our lives? Proverbs 1:29-31says,

What are some ways you can "trouble proof" your dating life and get the most enjoyment from it?

Purity is one of your most precious possessions.

Look up the word "pure" in the dictionary.

Once again, where does impurity begin? *It begins in your mind.* You must *guard* what you see, listen to, and allow your mind to think about.

The Internet and Pornography
Pornography is so easy to access with the Internet. Once you view something, it has passed the gate—your eyes—into your mind. Then it is there forever. The image is never to be erased. Satan would just love to fill your mind with filth.

Ted Bundy, a serial killer in the 1970s and 1980s, said his cruel murders of some thirty women and young girls all began with his desire to look at pornography. *Look online for a short video clip of part of James Dobson's death row interview with Ted Bundy.*

The popular television show *Dateline* shows sting operations of perverts preying on young women via the Internet. *This is nothing to play with!* Stay away from unwholesome websites.

I blame part of the problem of sexual permissiveness on my generation. We have been far too "tolerant" and have not sought and taught God's Word as instructed. Titus 2:3-5

Pearls of Wisdom from Proverbs

Proverbs 4:11-12:

Proverbs 4:23:

Proverbs 15:14:

Proverbs 19:23:

Song of the week: "He Leadeth Me" by Candi Pearson

LESSON 18

Any Vessel Can Be Used—the Story of Rahab

Read Joshua chapters 2 and 6. The main characters of this story are Joshua, Rahab, and the two spies.

1) Joshua was leading the Israelites into the promised land of _____.
2) He sent _____ into the city of _____, one of the most wicked cities.
3) Rahab was a _____ and lived on the outer wall to the city, a prime location for her occupation.
4) How do you think Rahab and the people of Jericho had heard of the Israelites before they reached Jericho? Joshua 2:10

5) Even in those early days, news of this magnitude would travel from city to city! What miraculous events are we told of in the journey of escape from Egypt?

Rahab had heard the stories of how God had helped the Israelites escape slavery and the miracles he had performed in the desert. Their story had **inspired** her and she chose to believe in God as well. When the spies entered her home she knew she could be killed for hiding them but chose rather to act on her new faith. She believed that God could spare her and her family if they were overtaken in an attack by the Israelites.

6) Joshua and the Israelites destroyed the city. What became of Rahab and her family?

At some moment in your life, you heard of God and his *love for you. You had to make a decision* to accept or to reject him. Your belief in God, just like Rahab's, can change your destiny. He can take any life, no matter what the situation, and turn it around. One great biblical example is Paul, a man who once hated and persecuted Christians. He later became a mighty man of God and authored much of the New Testament.

Matthew 1:5

Hebrews 11:31

James 2:25

Rahab received an extraordinary inheritance for her faith. How was she honored?

It doesn't matter what your limitations are or what your past is. It is not what the vessel is made of that matters; it is what fills it! If given the opportunity, God can direct a heart and use any of us, just like he did Rehab.

Matthew 10:8 reminds us that freely we have received and freely we should give.
There is no doubt that you can use this story many times in your life. When you have a friend who has sinned and feels like there is no hope, what a wonderful example Rahab could be.

Salvation, conversion, or trusting God can be broken down into three categories:

1) life before knowing God,
2) time of believing,
3) life after surrendering to God.

These three categories make up your Christian testimony.

Song of the week: "Basics of Life" by 4 Him

LESSON 19

PRAYER

"Let us then approach the throne of grace with confidence, so that we may receive mercy and find grace to help us in our time of need." Hebrews 4:16

When we pray, we connect to the awesome God who created this amazing universe. We can come to him at any time, day or night. He will not be asleep. His line will not be busy. We will not hear, "All of our operators are assisting other customers." What an incredible privilege we have to fellowship with an ever-available, loving heavenly Father and lay all our concerns before him.

Does it seem to you that some people have a closer connection with heaven than others? Do some people seem to have more prayers answered? Are there certain people you would want praying for you because you are sure they have a more direct hotline?

1) Can some people really pray more effectively than others? James 5:16b

The Bible tells us that all have sinned, and that no one is righteous. So how can we become righteous and have a more effective prayer life? II Corinthians 5:21 tells us that through Christ we can become right with God. He made this possible at the cross. We could say that the first condition for an effective prayer life is to belong to God by accepting Christ and having our sins forgiven.

2) Are all Christians able to pray effectively?
    Psalm 66:18

    Isaiah 59:2

3) God has made a provision for the Christian who has sinned. I John 1:9 has been called "the Christian's bar of soap." Write it here:

So if we want to pray effectively, we need to first confess our sins and allow God to cleanse us. When we ask God to reveal our sins and then confess them, he will cleanse us from all unrighteousness, even those things we may have forgotten or may not have recognized as sin. Not only does God forgive our sins, but he also forgets them. If we come to him and say, "Oh Lord, I've done it again," he will say, "Done what?"

We have seen two conditions for praying effectively: accepting Christ and keeping our sins confessed. There are also some other conditions that will enable us to pray even more effectively.

4) Read John 15:7

5) What does it mean to "remain in Christ?"

6) What does it mean for God's word to "remain in us?"

Most of us know more of God's principles than we are doing.

7) I John 3:22 underscores obedience and gives us another condition. What is it?

8) What could be the difference between keeping God's commandments and doing those things that are pleasing to him?

Another condition is faith! Mark 11:24

9) How can we increase our faith? Romans 10:17

As we trust God in situation after situation, we experience his faithfulness and come to rely on it every time. Our faith also grows as we share our lives with other Christians and are encouraged by seeing and hearing how God is working in their lives. *This is one of the benefits of Bible study!*

10) What is another condition of prayer that is found in James 4:3?

This may give insight as to why some of our prayers have not been answered. God may give us an answer to our prayers other than yes. He may say no, maybe, or wait and see. He may give us something much better than what we have requested. Someone has said, "God gives the best to those who leave the choice with him." If God isn't always going to give us what we ask for, why should we pray? James tells us, "We have not because we ask not." God is willing to give us many things if we but ask.

11) Is asking God for what we want the only reason to pray? What other reasons are there?

What an honor and privilege to be able to praise him, thank him, enjoy fellowship with him, and just "be still" and listen to what he has to say to you!

Song of the week: "Be Still and Know" by Steven Curtis Chapman

LESSON 20

FORGIVENESS

"Be kind and compassionate to one another,
forgiving each other, just as in Christ God forgave you." Ephesians 4:32

Unfortunately, people in our lives will sometimes say or do things that hurt us. How do you find yourself reacting when this happens to you?

What makes people be unkind to other people? It is really more about them and who they are trying to be than it is about you.

Does the Bible have things to say about forgiving those who have mistreated us? Is this an easy or hard thing to do?

Why Should We Forgive?

There are several reasons. The main reason is that Jesus told us to forgive, and that's reason enough by itself.

1) Read Matthew 18:21-22:

Do you think Jesus meant for us to count the times we've forgiven someone else and withhold forgiveness after so many times?

We should forgive others so God will forgive us. We pray in the Lord's Prayer, "Father, forgive us as we forgive those that trespass against us."

2) What do Matthew 6:14-15 and Luke 6:37 have to say on this subject?

We should forgive others so God will hear our prayers. Since God has told us to forgive offenses against us, unforgiveness is a sin.

3) These two verses tell us what about our sin of unforgiveness?

Psalm 66:18

Isaiah 59:2

When we have sin in our lives, God does not listen to us.

It has been said that acid can corrode the vessel that contains it. The person who is hurt most by an unforgiving attitude is not the one who has done wrong but the one who refuses to forgive. The person who has hurt us doesn't even realize we are thinking mean thoughts, but those thoughts steal our enjoyment of life. We can be at a fun party or a sleepover at our best friend's house, but the bitterness in our hearts takes away the pleasure we should have.

4) Hebrews 12:15 could help in this situation. Write it here

You may say, "I can forgive, but I can't forget." The memory of abuse from others does linger in our memory banks, but we have a choice. We can go over and over the details in our minds and feel the hurt all over again, or when we are tempted to do that, we can focus elsewhere, especially on God's grace and goodness to us. What is the hardest thing you have had to forgive?

I marvel at those who have *forgiven* the brutal, senseless murders of one of their loved ones. One example is the family of Rachel Scott, a teenager who was killed in the Columbine High School shooting. Here is their story entitled, "What Role Does Forgiveness Play in Overcoming Tragedy?" by Beth Nimmo and Darrell Scott (found in the *The Answer Bible*):

> People respond differently to tragedy when it strikes their lives. Some never get over it. Others become bitter and angry, and that is easily understandable. However, we are given the opportunity to experience a realm of grace that is incomprehensible to some when we choose to forgive. Were we angry when our daughter Rachel Scott was killed in the shootings at Columbine High School? Yes! Were we sad? Beyond description! But are we forgiving? That is probably one of the most difficult issues to face when you have been so deeply wronged.
>
> Our understanding of God's heart left us only one choice, the decision to forgive. It was the choice of Jesus as He hung on a cross dying. He said in Matthew 5:43-44: "You have heard that it was said, 'Love your neighbor and hate your enemy.' But I tell you: Love your enemies and pray for those who persecute you."

Forgiveness is not just for the offender. It is also for the one who is offended. If we do not forgive, we end up in perpetual anger and bitterness and eventually offend others with our words or actions. If we forgive, we experience a "letting go" or cleansing process that frees us from the offender.

There is a great misunderstanding about forgiveness. Forgiveness is not pardon. Forgiveness is an attitude, while pardon is an action. Had they lived, we would not have pardoned these boys for what they did. In fact, I (Darrell) would have killed them to prevent the slaughter that occurred if I had been given the chance. I believe most people would have done the same. If they had lived, we would have testified against them and demanded that justice be done. However, our hearts toward them could not have harbored unforgiveness. Unforgiveness blocks God's ability to flow through us to help others.

God wants us to overcome evil with good. Such a thing is beyond human ability, but it is possible when we acknowledge our weakness and submit to God's grace. *The Answer Bible* taken from *Rachel's Tears by Beth Nimmo and Darrell Scott* (Word Publishing, A Division of Thomas Nelson, 2003) p 1153.

Forgiveness is required of us if we are to live healthy, non-bitter, God-pleasing lives.

Song of the week: "Amazing Love" by Christine Young

LESSON 21

CONFIDENT LIVING

"For God did not give us a spirit of timidity, but a spirit of power, of love and of self-discipline." II Timothy 1:7

(My inspiration came from a sermon by my beloved pastor, Terry Greer, and I have used some of his illustrations.)

1) Read Romans 8:12-15. We as Christians are _____ by God! Does this give you comfort?

2) What is fear? *Use the dictionary!*

3) What are most people afraid of? Come up with a top ten list of your own.

1.

2.

3.

4.

5.

6.

7.

8.

9.

10.

People can be weighed down or even paralyzed by fear! It can drain your energy and take away your power. You can become unhappy and nonproductive.

4) Write out II Timothy 1:7:

5) How can you avoid fear and enjoy God's power? John 15:7 says,

6) How do you remain in Him?

As a teenage girl, I became curious about demon possession. The more I read about this subject (and I did use Christian resources), the more I opened my mind to the dealings of Satan, and the more afraid I became. One night my father came in my room and could sense my anxiousness and fear. He proceeded to throw away all the books and literature I had read. Then he prayed with me. He gave me some good advice that night when he told me to stop thinking about Satan and to concentrate on the things of Christ. I was not focusing on a healthy subject; this is one reason I discourage horror movies and some video games.

Power, Love and a Sound Mind!

Power

Ask God, relying on his infinite wisdom, to help you. You are speaking to the creator of the universe. Is any situation too large or small for him? The only power that can counteract fear is the power of faith. Pray before you face a fearful situation or when you are in one. Know that he can give you a "peace that passes all understanding." Also realize that you learn and grow spiritually by going through hard situations. Satan can be more powerful than we are, but God is more powerful than Satan.

I John 4:4

James 4:7

Love

There are different types of *love*. I believe this verse is referring to two kinds of love. The first is *storge* love, which gives needed support and care. This kind of love is shown in good times and bad. The other kind of love is *agape* love, an unconditional love that endures selflessly.

Sound Mind

What does it mean to have a *sound mind?* You don't depend upon emotions but rather use grounded, straight, logical thinking without prejudice. Think according to the facts. Sometimes you do not think this way because you are upset. What might you do in this situation?

7) How can an "unsound" mind develop?

Sometimes we tend to make "knee jerk" reactions without thinking things through! As Christians, we are to seek God's counsel first. We are to know Scripture so we can apply God's thoughts to our situations. When we react to fearful situations under our own power, sin usually results. Instead of responding with love, we tend to lash out or hold in feelings of hatred and bitterness.

Hebrews 12:15 instructs us to "pluck" bitterness out by the roots, never allowing it to grow. If we do not, our sins will fester and infect every aspect of our lives. They are a foreign substance to our bodies if we are believers.

How Do I Deal with This Kind of Fear?

There are 366 "Fear nots" in the Bible.

Is God showing you anything in your life from which you need to be freed?

Song of the week: "Fear Not" by Justin Davis

LESSON 22

HEAVEN

"For to me, to live is Christ and to die is gain. If I am to go on living in the body, this will mean fruitful labor for me. Yet what shall I choose? I do not know! I am torn between the two: I desire to depart and be with Christ, which is better by far;" Philippians 1:21-23

1) Where do we get our ideas about what heaven is like?

2) Are near-death experiences for real?

The Bible has over 582 references to heaven in some 550 verses.

3) Is heaven a real place? John 14:2-3

4) What does heaven look like? The apostle John was given a wonderful vision of heaven while he was in exile on an island called Patmos, and this is the fullest description we have of heaven in the Bible.

Revelation 4:3

Revelation 4:4

Revelation 4:6

Revelation 21:11-14, 19, 21

Heaven is a place of *"no mores."*

Revelation 21:3-4

Think about it . . .

A. No more sorrow, and no more tears.
B. No more sickness—doctors, hospitals, medicine, pain.
C. No more death—cemeteries, funerals.
D. No more crime—murder, jails, police. Revelation 21:27*"Nothing impure will ever enter it, nor will anyone who does what is shameful and deceitful, but only those whose names are written in the Lamb's Book of Life."*

John was separated from those he loved by the sea that surrounded the island of Patmos. In heaven we will be reunited with our loved ones, never to experience the pain and loneliness of being separated from them again. Is there someone you are looking forward very much to seeing in heaven?

5) Will we be angels in heaven, have wings, and play harps?

Psalm 8:4-5a

Hebrews 1:14

6) Will we be ourselves in heaven?

7) Explain 1 Corinthians 15:35-39

8) Will we have memories?

9) Will we know our loved ones in heaven, and will they know us?

Randy Alcorn in his book on heaven wrote, "If you study Jesus' interactions with Mary Magdalene, Thomas, and Peter, you will see how similar they are to His interactions with these same people before He died. The fact that Jesus picked up His relationships where they had left off is a foretaste of our own lives after we are resurrected. We will experience continuity between our current lives and our resurrected lives, with the same memories and relational histories." Randy Alcorn, *Heaven* (Carol Stream, IL: Tyndale House publishers, Inc., 2004) p 117.

Our parents will still be our parents, and our children will still be our children. One of the things we look most forward to in heaven is being reunited with family and friends who have gone on before us!

I Corinthians 2:9b

Heaven will be far greater and more wonderful than anything we could ever imagine! I wonder if there will be colors we have never seen or music notes we have never heard. Perhaps we will have more than five senses or travel through space. Who knows?

I believe we will have glorious worship services in heaven when we are finally face to face with our Lord and Savior!

I Timothy 6:17 tells us that God:

We can trust him to make heaven a wondrous place.

Song of the week: "There Will Be a Day" by Jeremy Camp